. . . I woke up!

And then . . .

I was crazy with fear! I cried, 'Oh please, please, please don't let it be a monster about to gobble me up!'

A slimy, flesh-eating monster.
With big, round, bulging, red eyes.
And a drooling mouth full of razor-sharp, yellow fangs.
And really smelly, hot breath.
And strong, hairy arms. With long, sharp claws, dripping blood.
A hideous monster ready to rip me apart and eat me up!

'What if, oh but please, please, please I hope it's not. But what if, it really is a MONSTER! A monster stuck down here with ME in this deep, dark, cold, and really smelly, wet hole!'

My mind started to think about those other nasty, horrible, yukky things again! Those things that I had been desperately trying not to think about. Only now it just wouldn't stop!

I thought, 'What if, just maybe, it isn't another human person at all? What if it isn't a boy? Or a girl? Or a man? Or a woman?'

'I want my mummy!' I cried.
But that time my voice didn't echo at all down that deep, dark, cold, and really smelly, wet hole!
That heavy, hollow breathing had slowly sploshed its way closer and closer and closer towards me and now I could feel it breathing hot and smelly right in my face!

Then I thought, 'Well maybe it could be any one of those people. Or maybe it could be all of them together.'
But I didn't really think so!

'Or please, please, please, let it be a soldier. A real tough-guy, armed to the teeth with knives, and guns, and bombs, and rocket launchers, and a tank. An enormous tank to take me right out of this deep, dark, cold, and really smelly, wet hole.'
'Just hurry up please!' I prayed.

23

Then my mind started to panic.
'Who else could it be? Who else could be stuck down here with me in this deep, dark, cold, and really smelly, wet hole?' I wondered.
'Perhaps it could be a policeman who has come looking for me?
Or my big, strong dad?
Or the man who cleans the drains?
Or a fireman wearing a breathing mask?
Or a jockey riding a race horse?
Or a puffed-out marathon runner?
Or a spaceman?
Or a whole herd of cattle?
Or a troop of boy scouts out for a walk?
Or a deep sea diver?
Or an eskimo on a sledge, pulled by twenty husky dogs?'

But nobody answered me!
Only that heavy, hollow breathing, slowly sploshing its way closer and closer and closer towards me!

I thought, 'Well maybe it could be grumpy, old Mrs Sharples and her yappy dog.'
But I didn't really think so!

With relief, I suddenly remembered about grumpy, old Mrs Sharples from next door. She sometimes breathes just like that, especially when she shouts at me for skating down her path!

Maybe Mrs Sharples had been out walking Nibbles, her yappy Yorkshire Terrier.

When suddenly . . . 'Oops!' Bash! Bonk! Sploosh!

She could have accidentally fallen down this deep, dark, cold, and really smelly, wet hole.

'Nibbles, come here boy' I whistled.

And I listened to the echo of my voice dying, down that deep, dark, cold, and really smelly, wet hole.

19

Then my mind started to play those nasty tricks on me again! Monsters and ghosts, ghouls and goblins, aliens and creepy crawlies, all danced around in my head!

'No! No! No! NO! NO!!' I said to myself.

But nobody answered me!
Only that heavy, hollow breathing, slowly sploshing its way closer and closer and closer towards me!

I thought, 'Well maybe it could be Lucy Loopin who had accidentally fallen down here.'
But I didn't really think so!

Perhaps the same thing had happened to Lucy?
'Oops!' Smack! Bang! Sploosh!
She could have accidentally pushed her pram straight into this deep, dark, cold, and really smelly, wet hole?
'Is that you Lucy?' I called, and my voice echoed into the deep, dark distance.

I thought, 'Well maybe it could be Simon on his new skateboard.'
But I didn't really think so!
'So if it isn't Simon, who else can it be?' I wondered, and I had to fight with my mind again, to make it stop thinking about those nasty, horrible, yukky things!
Then I remembered that little Lucy Loopin often pushed her toy pram up and down our street. She was always getting in my way.

I plucked up the courage to say something. But my throat was so dry that my voice just wouldn't come out! I swallowed hard and tried again.

'Er, is that you Simon?' I croaked, and my voice echoed down that deep, dark, cold, and really smelly, wet hole.

But nobody answered me!

Only that heavy, hollow breathing, slowly sploshing its way closer and closer and closer towards me!

Perhaps Simon had been skating along our street. And then . . . 'Oops!' Bonk! Wallop! Sploosh!
He had accidentally fallen down this deep, dark, cold, and really smelly, wet hole.

Then I thought, 'Perhaps it could just be another boy stuck down here with me in this deep, dark, cold, and really smelly, wet hole?'
I knew that my friend Simon had just been given a skateboard for his birthday. I hoped it was him.

The kind of things that make me hide my eyes when I watch a horror movie. Or the kind of things that lurk under my bed, waiting for the light to go out. Or the kind of things I sometimes frighten my baby sister with when Mum isn't looking!
'Stop it! Stop it! Stop it!' I said to myself. But it was really difficult!

I wondered, 'Who else could be stuck down here with me in this deep, dark, cold, and really smelly, wet hole?' Instantly, my mind started to think about all of those nasty, horrible, yukky things that I just didn't want it to think about!

I wanted to climb out of that deep dark, cold, and really smelly, wet hole but the sides were just too steep and slippery.
And I could still hear that heavy, hollow breathing, slowly sploshing its way closer and closer and closer towards me!

I was frightened out of my skates!
My knees were knocking. My teeth were chattering. My heart was thumping like a drum.
A hot flush wriggled its way down my spine and I shivered all over.

In . . . Out . . . In . . . Out.
Heavy, hollow breathing.
In . . . Out . . . In . . . Out.
And it was slowly sploshing around in the water, moving closer and closer and closer towards me!

It was deep. It was dark. It was cold. It was really smelly. And it was wet.
But worst of all, I knew that I was not alone!
There was something else down there with me in that deep, dark, cold, and really smelly, wet hole. I couldn't see what it was, but I could hear something breathing.

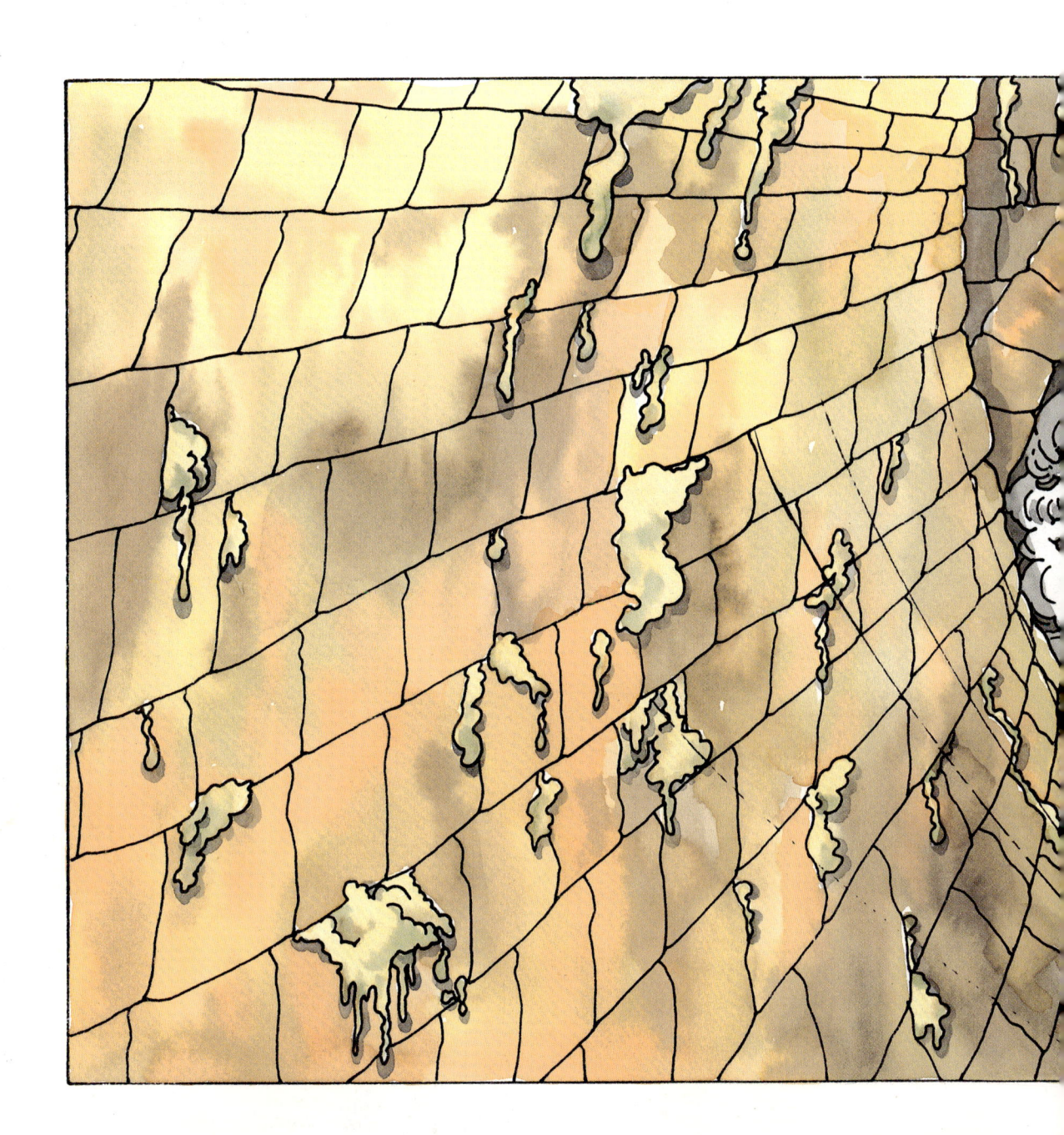

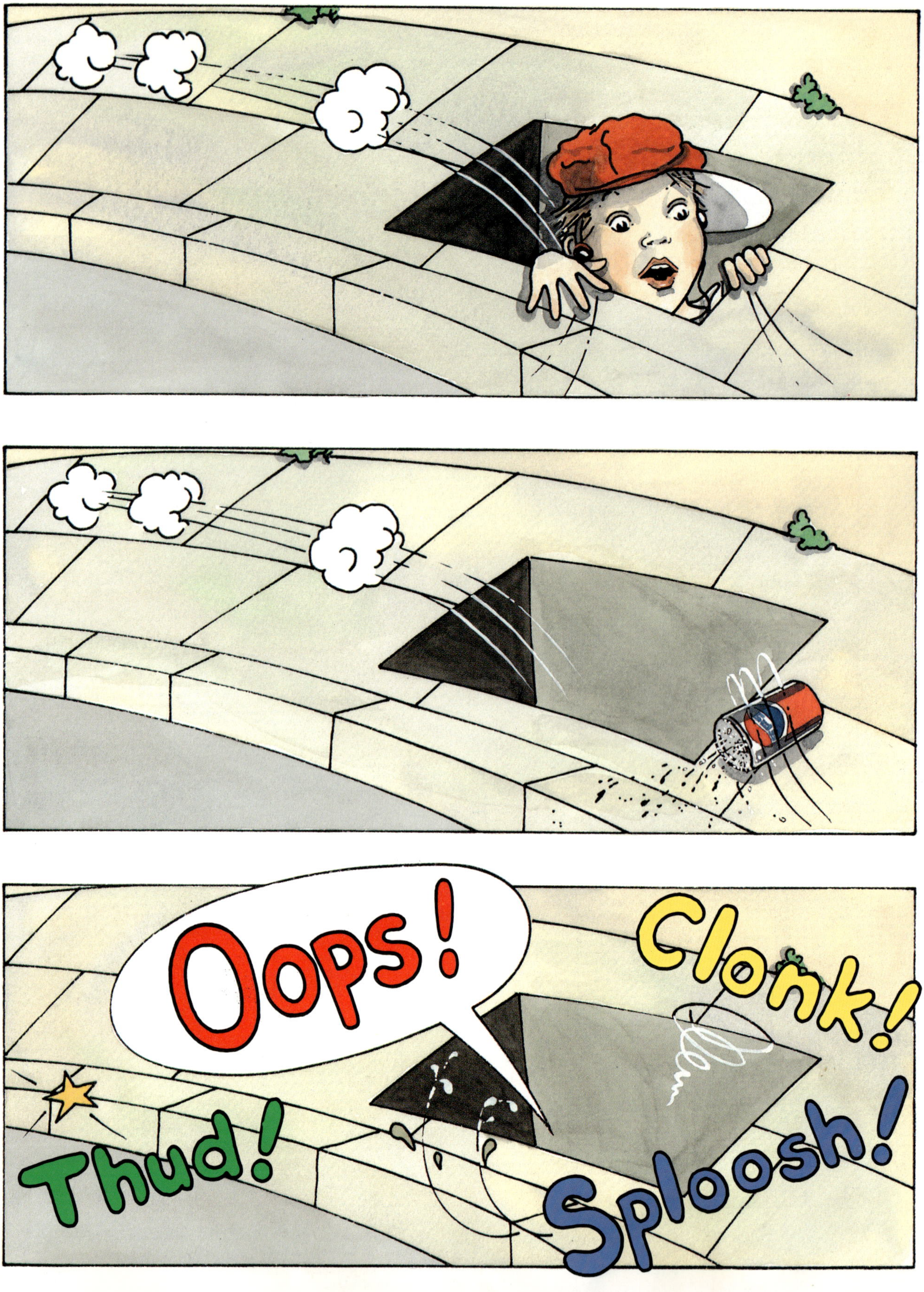
Oops!
Clonk!
Thud!
Sploosh!

And then suddenly, I fell straight down a man-hole!

3

It was very hot today.

I went skating along our street. Guzzling my favourite drink and listening to my favourite sounds. But I didn't look where I was going.

The Deep, Cold, and Really Smelly, Wet Hole

Ross Robertson

Illustrations by
Gloria